June 13, 1997

Delilah

I don't know if you will enjoy this, but I hope you do. It is part of my self that I only share with friends.

always
Hazel

Published by Vantage Press, Inc.
516 West 34th Street, New York, New York 10001

Manufactured in the United States of America
ISBN: 0-533-09718-5

Library of Congress Catalog Card No.: 91-91061

0 9 8 7 6 5 4 3 2 1

To Debra, for encouraging me to keep writing;
for Tiffany, for bringing the hidden child in me out;
and for my sister Mona, who always believed in me

Contents

The Mists

The mists that I see swirling round you and me
Are the mists of the love that we knew.
The sky that surrounds you and I is the sky—
That our love once knew, summer blue.
And I feel ever more the things we adored
When we walked hand in hand to the shore.
But our love is gone, and I don't know what's wrong
With the vow that we made long ago.
The mists that I see that swirled round you and me
Have been blown by the wind to the sky.
And now it's not you, it's not me, it's not us,
It's the loneliest word, it's just I.

Would You?

If I asked you to hold me
would you hold me real tight
until our bodies were one
and they disappeared in the light?
Would you tell me you loved me
and that I'm the only one
that you care for
and you live for
and that I am
your bright warm sun?

We Are One

I do not know what led me
to the door into your heart;
a look, a smile, your understanding
feelings from the start.
I tried to thwart the love
that you were building there,
but each rebuke just brought
you closer without fear.
I finally saw the care and love
within your eyes
and realized I loved you too,
to my surprise.
And now the feelings we once
held apart, alone,
are wrapped in love, between the
two of us, we're one.

4

Lost

I closed all the windows and boarded up the doors
for love I've found is fleeting,
and I can't find it anymore.
I wanted someone to love and need me
for just who I am,
not just a passing fancy—Do you understand?
I'm so tired of hearing,
"Someday he'll come along."
Someday hasn't happened,
I fear they were all wrong;
for all the kinds of love that God has handed out
I just wanted someone to love me
without a doubt.
To love me for a lifetime,
to share my hopes and dreams,
to hold me when I cried and laugh at my silly schemes,
to say, "You know I love you,
my life is useless without you."
But, God, I've lost that battle;
why am I one of those few?

Our Love

You have touched my heart, my love—
Returned the favors that I have never asked repaid.
Entwined your life around and into mine,
And held my secrets close unto your heart.
I am not worthy.
I've sensed the pain that I have given you,
And traced the tears that have fallen from your eyes.
But all and all, my intentions have been clear—
To keep you safe and near to me no matter what the cost.
For you and I are one within our universe—
And ecstasy and love are reflected in our eyes.

Because

I've opened my heart
even tunnels in my mind
those that led to vaults
of sadness hidden with time.
I've opened all the doors
that once were closed to light
and bared all the nerves that once
prodded me to fight.
I've torn down all the walls
that had me secluded inside;
I've even tempered
my high-minded pride.
And all this I have done
because I have found
that you love me, and care for me,
and my life you've turned around.

Repay

How can I ever repay you—are the words I start to say
But these words are not appropriate;
Repay is not the way.
What needs to be said has no words that define my feelings
    here
For the things that you have done for me are out of pure love
    and care.
What do you say to a friend who has given up their life
To be with you during all the bitter times and strife?
How do you say—you're special, wonderful, you're fine
You're thoughtful, you're caring, I'm glad, as a friend—you're
    mine.
How can I ever repay you—are the words I start to say
But these words are not appropriate;
Repay is not the way.

Come—Tempt Me

Come tempt me with all your foolish dreams
For "foolish" they are not
Come tease me with your accomplishments
And battles you have fought
Come bring me all your hopes and cares
And spread them all around
For we shall pick and choose of these
And Heaven shall you astound.

The Thorn and the Rose

Two people walked along two separate roads—
one a thorn and one a rose.
They stumbled, fought, but found in time
that both their roads would intertwine.
Then up ahead, they crossed, it seems—
one bringing hope, one bringing dreams.
And finding their roads ran parallel
the thorn and rose trod up the hill;
but coming down the rose did fall
its petals limp, its stem bent—no longer tall.
The thorn knelt down beside the rose
and gently held it high and froze.
On seeing this, God did decree
the thorn and rose should ever be;
the rose to bask in someone's dreams—
the thorn to protect its hopes and its schemes.
And like these two, we have become—
our friendship's hopes and dreams are one.

It Will Become Brighter

If you feel like the world
has backed off on you now
and the dreams that you dream
aren't important somehow.
Just remember I'm here
to stand tall at your side
and all of this will be brighter
with the new tide.
For like the ocean that roars in
from a far-off shore
bringing new life and treasures galore
a new day shall bring you
the dreams that you dream
and I'll be there to share all
your hopes and your schemes.

To Share Equally from the Heart

I laid my grief before you
on the table of my despair.
And let you pick and chose
of the hurt and pain that was there.
And yet, my friend, you surprised me
and took it all to heart.
You cradled all my hurting and pain
and of me—you became a part.
So it should not really amaze you
or take you back a step
when I ask for all your hurt and pain
and all the tears you have wept.
For friendship does not always mean
the same—but apart.
But friendship does mean
to share equally from the heart.

You're Always There

My friend, what can I say for all you've done for me.
My thoughts tumble, my feelings are jumbled,
my words lost on a foamy sea.
A treasure chest of things you have done
now creep into my mind—
and each time I turned around,
what wonders I did find.
Your kindness and your caring have not been lost, you see
nor has your love, nor your sharing,
nor your unselfish thoughts of me.

Self

When Self is all that I possess—
the essence of me, my mind,
all that I have I share with you, my friend,
for all time.
I cannot give you material things
for that is for others to do,
but in times of trouble, in times of pain,
in times when I am with you—
I'll share with you the Self I am—
the Self that longs to be free
the Self that few others have touched,
the Self that is only me.
And if you but choose to lock Self away—
in a corner of your mind—
releasing it only somewhere, far distant
down your life's line.
Then Self shall be content and warm
as I feel this day.
For somewhere, sometime, Self will be free
and out of harm's way.
For when I offer you my Self
from the bottom of my heart
there is nothing, nothing that one can do
to break Self apart.
When Self is all that I possess—
the essence of me—my mind;
all that I have I share with you
my friend—for all time.

Friends

It's the love and the caring
and the pure joy of sharing
all the pain and sorrow
and good times.

For our friendship has grown stronger
and my mind's alone no longer
whether you are here
or I am all alone.

From God's Hand

I watched a tiny glowing star come drifting
down from God's higher plane.
I caught that star and threw it out,
but it came back again.
God said, "This is friendship
and the brighter that it glows
is to remind you that friendship—
even through its woes—
is stronger than anything that
I have made out there
and friendship—like
my love for you—
is to cherish and to share."

Sharing

I came to you in friendship
but, God, I never knew
that friendship entailed more
than just being around you.
We have shared self for self,
pain for pain and laughter galore
but we have really shared
so very much more.
My pain is reflected in your eyes
and your pain is etched into my mind.
I feel a closeness that only real
friends do share.
But that's because we both do more
than just care.
If you ever need me,
as I have needed you
I would be there, my friend,
but this you already knew.

Roadblocks

It's not the dreams that we have
that tend to slow us down;
it's the roadblocks we place in front,
behind and all around.
So if we take a moment and
calm our minds a bit
we find that friends will help
make all the pieces fit.
So don't despair when dreams they shatter
and life seems all so hard
for two minds are better than one
when reaching for a star.

Friendship Measured

By what guide do you measure friendship?
A voice in a crowd urging you on
A person beside you when all is gone
Tears fall when you are sad
Smiles that follow when you are glad
Friendship measured, by what?
An understanding heart
A kind word, or a friendly
smile from the start.

We Seldom Say . . .

Apart from all the other things
that flitter through my mind—
my home, my family, the important
things that take up all my time—
I think of you, my friend
who have shared all my secret dreams
who have been there when it really mattered
who have bolstered all my crazy schemes.
We seldom say to each other
we love, we care, we miss;
but God had us both in mind
when He sent us friendship's bliss.
Apart from all the other things
that flitter through my mind;
you, my precious friend
are with me all the time.

Friends Are Always There for Us

If I could see what you are thinking
when your eyes go gray with pain
and your tears they fall so quickly
like a downpour of winter rain.

If I could touch the heart that's in you
and ease the ache that's there
and even make you laugh when
you feel that you no longer care.

If I could just reach out and
touch you and say you are my friend
all this pain that you are feeling
we both could understand.

But sometimes, my friend, you slip
away to some uncharted isle
keeping feelings and hurt penned up
like that little girl, that child.

And I long to say, come here to me
don't sit in silence now
for you are my friend, I care deeply
and we shall work this out somehow.

So I'll just say, my friend, no
matter where you are
if you ever need me, for anything,
I'm really not that far.

Never Alone

My friend, is it life that is unfair—
or is it just that empty chair
that sits across from me when I'm alone?
Is it you that I miss
or this hollow empty abyss
that I am forced to occupy when I'm at home?
You are sitting, laughing, crying
oh, my mind—is it lying?
You're not here for you have gone away.
All the pain and hurt inside us
has disbursed as did the shyness
when we first began to talk and share our days.
Now I've relearned love and caring
and the friendship that's worth wearing
on our shirtsleeves in the light of day.
For, my dear friend, God was not joking
when he set us into poking into each
nook and cranny of our minds.
It's the love and the caring
and the pure joy of sharing
all the pain and sorrow and good times.
For our friendship has grown stronger,
and our minds are alone no longer
whether you are here or I am all alone.

If I Chance . . .

If I chance to give you part of me—
some of my thoughts and dreams
would you handle them lovingly
like separating the milk from the cream?
Would you take all my thoughts in tow
and listen to what I've really said?
Would you cradle my dreams in your heart
and assure me I've nothing to dread?
If I chance to give you part of me—
some of my thoughts and dreams
would you handle them lovingly
as you are my friend—believe.

When I Can Talk

Oh, how happy I will be when I can talk
I'll tell Mommy and Daddy just how it feels not to crawl
    around, but to walk.
We'll sit around and talk of things so nice
At night I'll say my prayers out loud and bless my parents
    twice
I'll run in all the sunshine I can find
And scream to all the world, "Hey, look, this voice is mine."
And then I'll turn and look into the sky—
And tell God how wonderful He is and why.

Tiffany

I met this little girl today
that kind of blew my mind
with blonde hair and blue eyes
that sparkle—no, they shine.
She seems at times to be hiding
a grown-up girl inside
for just like her mother
she is full of love and pride.
When she is grown and reaches out
for her favorite star
I know God will reach out too,
so she won't have to reach so far.
She has her mother's temperment
and smile, that's plain to see
her name fits so beautifully,
because it's Tiffany.

I'm Proud to Be "I"

It's hard to be a winner
in someone else's eyes
when they keep telling you
you're not that great a prize.
But you see—when I was younger—
about the age of you
I had the same problems,
not with one person, but a few.
I began to fight back
the only way I knew how
but sometimes their cruel words
still hurt me now.
So I learned a great lesson
over the years;
I refuse to get upset
and cry any more tears.
For I found I am special,
I'm one of a kind
and you, like me,
will soon find
that no matter who bullies
or talks bad to you
you can say, "Hey—I have something
that's given to only a few
I have love and warmth,
and a heart as big as the sky
and you have to stay you,
But I'm Proud to be 'I' ".

My Cat Igers

(Ignoramus)

Our gray cat's a huge ole cat
he's fat and furry and round;
he takes control of all of us
with his tail up and eyes big like a clown.
He waits for Mom to come home
and greets her nose to nose.
He's my ole cat, and he's her ole cat
and he keeps us on our toes.
I love my cat, he's so round and fat
and he has blue eyes almost like mine
and his purr—oh, his purr
is so loud and deep and fine.

29

The Child

Chases the shadows of clouds across a field
Marvels at a butterfly a cocoon yields
Smells a flower so soft and red
Dreads the time set for bed.
Plays cowboys and Indians or house sometimes
And loves to listen to stories and rhymes
This is a world that used to be—
Long ago for people like you and me.

My Un-Poem

I tried to write you here a poem
But the words they did not fit
I pushed and shoved and altered things
But I slowly ran out of wit
The words were scrambled within my mind
And the pictures would not come
So this poem I wrote for you today,
Is, well—just a little bit dumb.

Part Four

Self

It's Free

To encase yourself in walls of stone
and never let one in,
to bind your heart so tightly
that you lose when you should win.
To hold in tears and fight
the hurt and stifle all the pain;
to be, but not to be, to live
but go insane.
To refuse a hand held out to you,
to ignore the care, the love;
is to close your eyes to God, my dear—
for it's free from heaven above.

I Ponder . . .

I ponder whether life and death
is just a foolish game;
a mystical illusion
to ease an old Roman God's pain;
a fantasy, if you wish,
to please a broken heart;
a misty memory in some
dark, cool green park.

But after all the pondering
and after all the dreams
I find that life and death
is as real as it seems.
It tends to shatter great
strong hearts and tear them apart;
it challenges the minds of many
people from the start.

If God had not made heaven and earth,
I must agree—
that you and I and all these
people would not be.
But then our illusions and our dreams
would not exist at all;
I wonder, my friend, is it worth it,
or an illusion we recall?

Dreaming

In my mind I'm sitting
on a far-off distant shore
feeling and having thoughts
I've never had before.
The ocean tide comes rolling in,
and spills between the rocks;
the ocean mist seeps into
and embraces all my thoughts.
I'm calmer now, and I can see
the fool that has been me;
a trace—a hint of courage
and my soul begging to be free.
I feel the arms of solitude
pressing close upon my mind,
the arms that are so comforting
in my world of twirling time.

I Feel

I base my suffering on moonlight and the light of day, willing
to concede that humanity has shocked my soul into
nothingness.
I come to think of life as a necessity to bring meaning to God's
existence in the universe.
Of all the things I cherish most, the closeness of a friend and
family, who do not doubt my being.
And whether you believe in me or not, my love for you
remains the same.
For friends and family they do not have to part when
thoughts ascend to different plains; and life exists and
goes on, no matter the terror that we feel.
But do honor to our friendship in the light and hold your
thoughts and beliefs above all.
For the suffering and chaos that have touched our souls
cannot deplete our willingness to strive for better things
in the darkness and the light.
And if you see a trace of tears behind my eyes, floating
endlessly in darkness, please, do not be surprised.
For God has touched me here and there with sufferings, and I
must fight to control these small damp things.

Reality

Precious time to hold onto one's Self
and thoughts that bide their time
in infinitesimal cocoons
in hallways of our minds.
A treasure chest of dreams we dreamt
and hopes are scattered there
among the webs and ghostly faces
floating in the air.
We chance to reach out when we dare
along those darkened walls
and touch the dreams that we have dreamt
and faces we recall.
But life screams . . . REALITY,
return unto my world.
For precious time and thoughts abide
in misty, life-colored swirls.

To Be Free

If God would have made me
as free as I'd like to be
and put no limitations
on my soul on life's sea
I would have been a vagabond
loving when I could
giving and taking, as you would.
I would swim the open seas of eyes
and ride the carefree minds;
I would tiptoe through private thoughts
of people lost in time.

My Dreams

I left my dreams in dark damp halls
Where dust and lonely spirits dwell
Touched by the stirring wind—that's all
And memories of times that fell

But once I tried to walk those halls
Retracing footsteps in the dust
I felt the vibration of a child's call
The lonely weeping—the toys turned to rust

The life I had known was there no more
The precious dreams were gone
All but diminished on a far-off shore
Like a haunting, beautiful song.